The 30-Day

Husband

Encouragement

CHALLENGE

Revive Our Hearts™

The 30-Day Husband Encouragement Challenge

Published by *Revive Our Hearts*
P.O. Box 2000
Niles, MI 49120

© 2020 *Revive Our Hearts*

Printed in the United States of America.

ISBN: 978-1-934718-77-3

Edited by Mindy Kroesche and Hayley Mullins.
Design by Austin Collins.

Emphasis in Scripture quotations added by the authors.

Table of Contents

Welcome

to the 30-Day Husband Encouragement Challenge!

It didn't take many weeks of marriage to Robert for me to learn that my attitudes and words have a profound effect on my husband. I have the ability to make Robert feel encouraged and cherished. But I also have the ability—more than any other person in his life—to deflate and discourage him.

We all need honest input from those who know us best and can help us see blind spots we may be oblivious to. But our ability to give humble, helpful critique and have it be well-received is in direct proportion to the effort we make to give the gift of encouragement.

Knowing how important (and neglected) this gift is in many marriages, I have often urged wives to take the 30-Day Husband Encouragement Challenge. Thousands of women have written to share with me how this simple exercise changed their heart toward their husband. Many have also shared how it changed their husband's heart toward them.

The challenge has two parts:

1. *For the next thirty days, don't say anything negative about your husband* to him or to anyone else about him.

2. *Each day, for the next thirty days, tell your husband something you admire or appreciate about him*—and say it to someone else about him!

Starting tomorrow, for the next thirty days, you'll read a Scripture verse, a short devotional from one of our *Revive Our Hearts* staff members or bloggers, and reflection questions—all designed to help you plant seeds of grace and encouragement in your relationship with your husband. Each day will also include a response from someone who took this challenge and saw the difference it made in her life and marriage.

On a scale of one to ten, your marriage may be at a negative two right now. Or maybe things are going well but there's room for improvement (as there always is!). This little challenge is probably not going to give your relationship an overhaul overnight. But if you'll stick with it for the next thirty days, I believe it will change you. And in time, as you water the soil of your husband's heart with affirmation and appreciation, you may see him change as well. Either way, you can't go wrong.

May the Lord encourage you as you encourage your man!

Nancy

Nancy DeMoss Wolgemuth

The 30-Day

Husband

Encouragement

CHALLENGE

The heart of her husband
trusts in her, and he will have
no lack of gain. She does him
good, and not harm, all the
days of her life.

—Proverbs 31:11–12

Day 1

Voice Your Gratitude

YOUR CHALLENGE:

- Don't say anything negative about your husband—to him or to anyone else about him.

- Tell your husband something you admire or appreciate about him—and say it to someone else about him!

VERSE

The heart of her husband trusts in her, and he will have no lack of gain. She does him good, and not harm, all the days of her life. — Proverbs 31:11–12

DEVOTIONAL

I'll never forget the day my husband proposed. I was on cloud nine because this man I loved so much had just asked me to be his wife! Now, twenty years later, there are still days I'm amazed I get to do life with him. But there are also moments of frustration, annoyance, or taking him for granted.

With over 7 billion people on our planet, have you ever considered the wonder of two people choosing to join their lives together in marriage? Out of all the women in the world, your husband chose to commit himself to you. He found you attractive as a person and appreciated you. Have you ever thanked him for it?

Though circumstances in your marriage may have changed since the day you said, "I do," it's important to let your husband know you're glad God brought you together and you want to be a blessing to him. Make sure he knows he can trust you to be in his corner and support him—no matter what.

—M.F.

PRAYER

Heavenly Father, I want to do good to my husband by encouraging him for the next thirty days. Soften my heart toward him, and show me how to voice my gratitude better. Teach me how to be in his corner so I can be his biggest supporter.

THE FRUIT OF ENCOURAGEMENT

"I'm seeing my husband light up when I'm specifically positive about his gifts and service. I'm feeling more harmony—tremendously so—in our home. I'm even surprised to hear my husband verbally encourage *me* more. It's contagious!"

REFLECT AND RESPOND

Do you remember how you felt when your husband first proposed?

_____

_____

How can you recapture that feeling as you go through the day-to-day of marriage?

_____

_____

What are some reasons you're thankful for your husband? How can you express that gratitude to him today?

_____

_____

How can you specifically show your husband that you support him?

_____

_____

GO DEEPER

One of the best opportunities to express gratitude is first thing in the morning. How do you greet your husband each morning? What's one way you can assure him of your love at the start of the day?

_____

_____

_____

_____

Lord Jesus, thank You for my husband. Give me the humility that's needed to notice evidence of Your grace in his life.

Day 2

Look for His Servant's Heart

YOUR CHALLENGE:

- Don't say anything negative about your husband—to him or to anyone else about him.

- Tell your husband something you admire or appreciate about him—and say it to someone else about him!

VERSE

Through love serve one another. —Galatians 5:13

DEVOTIONAL

One of the sinful tendencies of our hearts is to lack gratitude. If we neglect to appreciate the evidence of grace around us (and it becomes a habit), we slowly start to take everything for granted. One area where I need to be diligent in gratitude is in appreciating my husband's service to our family. I can quickly get used to his involvement in housework or with our children and then lose the opportunity to express how much I value his servant's heart.

Don't let ingratitude blind you to your husband's acts of service. Be on the lookout today for the small ways he shows his love for you and your family. Thank him and let him know how valuable his service is to you.

—B.G.

PRAYER

Lord Jesus, thank You for my husband. Give me humility that's needed to notice evidence of Your grace in his life. Open my eyes to the many ways he serves our family and others, and give me the joy of celebrating them. I pray with hope, knowing that You are the greatest servant.

THE FRUIT OF ENCOURAGEMENT

"I just started the challenge three days ago, and already I'm seeing change—in both my husband and me! I told my husband last night that this challenge has helped me recognize that he had a servant's heart and that I was sorry for not noticing on my own. His face lit up and a smile came across his face!"

REFLECT AND RESPOND

Do you frequently remind your husband of undone tasks around the house? If so, how can you point to ways he serves your family instead?

_____

_____

_____

_____

How does finding your satisfaction in Jesus alone lead you to be grateful toward others?

_____

_____

_____

_____

_____

How can you make it a habit to end your day with gratitude for your husband?

_____

_____

_____

GO DEEPER

Think of ways you could thank your husband for his servant's heart. If you have children, involve them in this exercise and make gratitude a family core value. Write him a note or thank him in public, but most of all, ask the Lord to give you a grateful heart.

" Adjust your perspective
and expectations. Only God
can meet the deepest needs
of your heart. "

Day 3

Cultivate Patience toward Your Husband

YOUR CHALLENGE:

- Don't say anything negative about your husband—to him or to anyone else about him.

- Tell your husband something you admire or appreciate about him—and say it to someone else about him!

VERSE

Whoever is slow to anger is better than the mighty, and he who rules his spirit than he who takes a city. —*Proverbs 16:32*

DEVOTIONAL

Patience is better than power? Yes. Patience—waiting with a good attitude or refraining from criticizing—can produce more desirable results and edify your husband in ways that exerting power never could. You can cultivate patience with your husband by allowing the Holy Spirit to control your reactions and emotions in the midst of a frustrating, annoying, or tedious situation. That Holy Spirit control is necessary for your heart, mind, and mouth.

For the momentary patience you need and the difficult, long-term waiting that you may be enduring, patience can act as a soothing salve. So, when your eyes want to bulge from seeing your husband do something "the wrong way" or you want to give up on waiting for a change, choose patience instead.

—*H.J.F*

PRAYER

Lord, Your divine power gives us everything we need for life and godliness, including patience. I surrender my selfish thoughts and desires to You. In their place, I ask that the Holy Spirit would take control of my mind, heart, and mouth so that I might have the patience and endurance I need with my husband. Build patience in me so that I might build up my husband.

THE FRUIT OF ENCOURAGEMENT

"Before this challenge, my husband was cold, distant and barely talking to me. I didn't want to talk to him, let alone encourage him, and I couldn't find anything about him to encourage. Through this challenge and prayer, I have seen my husband's attitude change toward me drastically. He now does little things for me and around the house that he would rarely do, and he is more open to me. Our relationship has grown so much that it has helped me to see the gem I have in my husband and to appreciate him even more."

REFLECT AND RESPOND

How can you make it a habit to assume the best of your husband before jumping to conclusions?

_____

_____

_____

_____

_____

What small act of patience can you do today that might grow your patience for more difficult circumstances?

_____

_____

_____

_____

GO DEEPER

Adjust your perspective and expectations. Your way and your desires are not ultimate; God's are. Seek to know more of Him so that your mind and heart will be shaped by Him. Only God can meet the deepest needs of your heart.

"
Even if your encouragement
to your husband starts small,
God can turn it to something
more than you can ever
imagine or think!

Day 4

Praise Your Husband's Work

YOUR CHALLENGE:

- Don't say anything negative about your husband—to him or to anyone else about him.

- Tell your husband something you admire or appreciate about him—and say it to someone else about him!

VERSE

Let him labor, doing honest work with his own hands. —Ephesians 4:28

DEVOTIONAL

During our eighteen-plus years of marriage, my husband has worked as a youth pastor, a UPS package handler, a church planter, an exterminator, a pastor, a substitute teacher, and in other smaller jobs, many times working two or three of them at once.

Maybe you can relate to this, or maybe your husband has worked the same job since he entered the workforce. Maybe you just wish your husband could find a job, any job. Regardless of our situations, we must look for ways to encourage our husbands in their work.

God has uniquely designed men to bear His image. They seem to be hardwired with a strong, inherent drive to provide. One of the most discouraging things a wife can do is to belittle her husband in this area that's right at the core of his masculinity. Complaining about his hours or his paycheck or nagging him to do more or better will drag him down. Instead, look for ways to build him up. Thank him for the work he does.

If he's unemployed, praise the qualities you see in him that make him a good worker. Let him know you respect him for working hard in any context that you see it.

—M.H.

PRAYER

Jesus, thank You for the way You've shaped and gifted my husband for the work he is able to do. Help me to support his work and praise him specifically for what he does. Plant in him a vision for how his gifts will build Your kingdom and serve others. Impress upon him the desire to be faithful with his gifts and use them fully. Protect him from discouragement, stress, dishonesty, and sluggishness so that he might bring praise to Your name.

THE FRUIT OF ENCOURAGEMENT

"I am married to an unbeliever, and at first it was hard for me to think of things I could encourage and appreciate about him. I asked God to let me see my husband with His eyes and, oh, did He! I thank my husband for the little things he does do, like take out the trash, grabbing something from the store on the way home, etc. Now I am able to see the important things he *does* for me, which makes me admire him even more. Even if your encouragement to your husband starts small, God can turn it to something more than you can ever imagine or think!"

REFLECT AND RESPOND

When is the last time you thanked your husband for doing his job and providing for the family?

_____

_____

_____

_____

What are some qualities you see in your husband that make him a good worker? For example, is he persistent? Honest? Dependable? Creative? Responsible?

_____

_____

_____

_____

GO DEEPER

Make it a point to thank your husband for his work. If this is an area of frustration in your marriage, it may be difficult to find ways to encourage your husband. Ask the Lord to show you specific qualities in your husband that you can honestly praise.

Christ would have you catch those sinful tendencies before they go from thoughts to words. Ask the Holy Spirit to guard your tongue.

Day 5

What's on Your Tongue?

YOUR CHALLENGE:

- Don't say anything negative about your husband—to him or to anyone else about him.

- Tell your husband something you admire or appreciate about him—and say it to someone else about him!

VERSE

Let no corrupting talk come out of your mouths, but only such as is good for building up, as fits the occasion, that it may give grace to those who hear. —Ephesians 4:29

DEVOTIONAL

Whether your husband is following hard after Jesus or is an unbeliever, it can be easy to see his sin and weakness. And it's easy in your own sin and weakness to use your words to tear Him down. But Christ would have you catch those sinful tendencies before they go from *thoughts* to *words.*

Ask the Holy Spirit to guard your tongue. Even when it's good and right to draw attention to sin or error in your husband's life, you can choose words that come from a humble heart and fit the situation to build him up. Choose to show him the same grace that you want him to show you. However, showing grace doesn't mean that you coddle or ignore sin; instead, it means you build up the hearer even when you have to confront a grievance.

Notice the thoughts that come to mind today about your husband. Before you let words come out of your mouth, consider whether what you want to say comes from a sinful desire to rule over him or from a desire to build him up. Deal with your own sin of pride first. Ask God for humility to speak with your husband about what's concerning you and for wisdom to find fitting words to build him up.

—S.D.

PRAYER

Father, I confess that I've torn down my husband with my words. I ask for Your forgiveness. Help me to look for fitting times to speak words that bring grace to my husband's ears. Help me not to ignore or coddle his sin but to deal with my own sin first so I can speak with my husband in humility and grace in a way that builds him up.

THE FRUIT OF ENCOURAGEMENT

"On Day 17, my husband surprised me with this statement. 'Honey, I've been a hard man and I don't need to be like that to you. I know nobody would stay with me, except you. Will you forgive me?' Wow! I was so touched by his sincerity and love. Not only has this challenge changed my husband, but it has changed me, too. It helps me to be mindful of how I should act toward him and be careful of what I say."

REFLECTION QUESTIONS

What bothers you the most about your husband?

_____

_____

_____

Is it really sin in him that bothers you or just idiosyncrasies or differences of opinion?

_____

_____

_____

How do you want your husband to approach you about your own sin? How can you model that approach?

_____

_____

_____

GO DEEPER

How are things going so far in the challenge? Even if you're not seeing changes, don't give up! Keep looking for ways to encourage your husband, and pray that the Lord will do "far more abundantly than all that we ask or think" (Eph. 3:20).

Spend some time today focusing on the words you use with your husband. If you tend to use your words to tear him down, focus on confessing this sin to God before you say a word to your husband. First tell him the good you see in him. Then, at the right time and with words of grace, address your concerns in such a way that your husband knows you're on his side.

"

Does your husband's
creative side have something
to teach you about the
character of God?

"

Day 6

Celebrate His Creativity

YOUR CHALLENGE:

- Don't say anything negative about your husband—to him or to anyone else about him.

- Tell your husband something you admire or appreciate about him—and say it to someone else about him!

VERSE

Whatever you do, do all to the glory of God. —1 Corinthians 10:31

DEVOTIONAL

My husband is a true craftsman. He is energized by a fine hide of leather or a perfect plank of wood. His mind is always working ten steps ahead, considering what he will build next. I admire this about him, but I admit I haven't always.

He is a man of many hobbies and talents; I tend to be more of a one-trick pony.

He values creative expression, an often messy and open-ended process; I tend to prioritize systematically ticking items off my to-do list. He likes things done right; I just want them to get done.

But I've learned to adore my husband's creative side because I see it as a way my husband bears the image of God.

God is infinitely creative. He paints sunrises and sunsets in thousands of shades of color. He made over 10,000 species of birds.

He carved giant mountains out of stone and sparkling diamonds out of carbon. No doubt the process of creation is never-ending and sometimes messy, yet aren't we grateful we love and serve a creative God?

Be on the lookout for your husband's creative side. Does he carve, build, or paint? Does he tinker on cars or strum a guitar? Let him know that you notice and appreciate the ways he is different than you in this area, and consider: does your husband's creative side have something to teach you about the character of God?

—E.D.

PRAYER

Heavenly Father, show me how You have wired my husband to reflect Your creative heart. Teach me to be an encouragement as he uses his gifts and talents to solve problems, serve others, and advance the kingdom. Thank You for revealing Your creativity through my husband for Your glory!

THE FRUIT OF ENCOURAGEMENT

"This challenge has been a blessing, not just in my marriage but for me on a personal level. My husband has been so much more in tune and loving to me. At first I was not going to do the challenge, but it has opened up my awareness of my responsibility as a wife to always esteem and say good things to and about my husband. It has changed the atmosphere in my home."

REFLECT AND RESPOND

In what ways is your husband creative?

_____

_____

_____

_____

_____

_____

Do you tend to encourage or discourage your husband's creative tendencies?

_____

_____

_____

_____

_____

_____

GO DEEPER

Do you recognize and appreciate your husband's creativity? Or do you criticize and demean his efforts? Instead of being negative, determine to be positive. Make his day by publicly praising his accomplishments while he is listening.

> Bless my husband with a wise heart that longs to honor You with everything we own.

Day 7

United on the Financial Front

YOUR CHALLENGE:

- Don't say anything negative about your husband—to him or to anyone else about him.

- Tell your husband something you admire or appreciate about him—and say it to someone else about him!

VERSE

I walk in the way of righteousness, in the paths of justice, granting an inheritance to those who love me, and filling their treasuries.
—*Proverbs 8:20–21*

DEVOTIONAL

Financial stress is often an occasion for disunity and distrust in our marriages. There are many fears and worries attached to money— or the lack of it—so it can become a very heated and hurtful topic. This challenge isn't about strengthening our finances, however, but our marriages. Sometimes to do the latter we need to set aside our goals for the former.

I'm not advocating that you cast aside all wisdom regarding your finances. But I am asking: are you willing to encourage your husband to lead in this area, even if it means that he makes some mistakes or doesn't value the things you think he should?

Today, tell your husband you trust his leadership in your finances. Look for ways to praise him in this area. Is he frugal? Does he live within a budget? Is he generous? Does he make wise investments? Is he thinking about the future? Tell him you appreciate these qualities and, if you need to, apologize for any negative comments you've made. If he's weak in this area, pray for him and look for ways to be helpful, not manipulative. Organize files or bills, and ask him how you can help.

—K.N.

PRAYER

Father, give me the strength to trust and submit to my husband, knowing ultimately You will take care of our family. Teach me to thank, encourage, and help my husband rather than criticize, complain, and hinder. Make us united in our financial decisions, even if it means You need to change me first. Bless my husband with a wise heart that longs to honor You with everything we own.

THE FRUIT OF ENCOURAGEMENT

"There were a couple of things I had wanted my husband to do for months before I started the challenge. One was to cut down on video games. The other was to handle a problem with our finances. I didn't want to nag, so I decided to let them go until the challenge was over. Well, God definitely showed up! On Day 1, my husband decided to cut out all video games and put his PlayStation away. He hasn't played video games in over a month. And this week, right after the challenge ended, he has taken the initiative to work out our financial situation on his own, which is a huge burden lifted off me. Praise God!"

Do you support or hinder your family's financial stability?

_____

_____

_____

_____

_____

_____

Are any of your financial disagreements rooted in personal preference? If so, how can you set aside your preferences and encourage your husband to lead?

_____

_____

_____

_____

_____

_____

GO DEEPER

Whether your husband is strong or weak in financial matters, you can strengthen your financial front by encouraging him in what he does well and giving him grace where he's weak. Ask how you can best help him in this area. Decide today not to respond with criticism and despair the next time you face a disagreement but rather with grace and hope.

Trust that even in your
darkest pain, God remains
faithful and true.

Day 8

Planting Faithfulness

YOUR CHALLENGE:

- Don't say anything negative about your husband—to him or to anyone else about him.

- Tell your husband something you admire or appreciate about him—and say it to someone else about him!

VERSE

A faithful man who can find? —*Proverbs 20:6*

DEVOTIONAL

Thousands of years ago, the writer of Proverbs 20 acknowledged faithfulness as a rare quality, and it's no different now. Our culture excuses and even encourages unfaithfulness. Many times, a man may feel like he's fighting a lonely battle to remain faithful to his marriage, his Lord, and his commitments in general.

As a wife, you can plant seeds of faithfulness in the heart of your husband. You can be his cheerleader to keep fighting and not give up. You can be a place of grace for him to turn when he is struggling against temptation. You can gently speak Truth to him when he is discouraged. And if he stumbles, you can receive him with mercy and forgiveness when he repents.

You may be reading this with a heart broken by your husband's unfaithfulness. If so, please seek out godly counsel to help you discern how to respond biblically. Trust that even in your darkest pain, God remains faithful and true.

Another important way to encourage your husband to faithfulness is to remain faithful yourself. May you rest on the grace of Christ to walk in faithfulness to Him and to your husband.

—M.H.

PRAYER

Lord Jesus, cultivate a faithful heart within my husband, one that longs to beat with integrity and flow with sacrificial love. Show me how I can plant seeds of faithfulness through my actions and attitudes toward my husband, and help me to wait on Your harvest in his heart.

THE FRUIT OF ENCOURAGEMENT

"Before this challenge, we had a 'rocky' marriage; it was really bad. There was yelling and name-calling and we constantly fought over stupid, small stuff. In just two days, I see us rekindling the relationship we had before all of the garbage we allowed between us."

REFLECT AND RESPOND

In what ways do you see faithfulness evident in your husband?

_____

_____

_____

_____

_____

_____

_____

Do you exhibit faithfulness in your own life? Are you a woman of your word?

_____

_____

_____

_____

GO DEEPER

Start watching for evidence of faithfulness in your husband, and point it out specifically when you find it. Let him know how much you appreciate his integrity and faithfulness. Write him a letter thanking him for his faithfulness to you in the midst of an unfaithful culture.

Lord Jesus, open my ears
to truly hear my husband.
Awaken my curiosity for
all the unspoken treasures
hidden in his heart and soul.

Day 9

Take Time to Listen

YOUR CHALLENGE:

- Don't say anything negative about your husband—to him or to anyone else about him.

- Tell your husband something you admire or appreciate about him—and say it to someone else about him!

VERSE

Be quick to hear, slow to speak. —James 1:19

DEVOTIONAL

When my husband took a class on biblical counseling, one of his assignments was for us to attend a counseling session with his teacher. The purpose was for him to be on the counselee side and learn from the process. Everything went well—until the end. At that moment, the counselor looked me in the eye and said, "Have you noticed you don't let this man speak?" I froze, and my husband said (with the best of intentions), "But I don't even realize it." The counselor replied, "That's the problem!"

In that moment I realized I was not being intentional in cultivating silence as a demonstration of love toward my husband. Something that seemed very simple required genuine repentance because a chatty mouth can be evidence of a proud heart. Now every day is a new opportunity to love my husband through silence with a heart that is ready to listen.

On this day, ask the Lord to show you if there is any trace of sin for which you need to repent. Surrender your desire to speak, and give your silence and attention to your husband as an expression of your love for him.

—B.G.

PRAYER

Lord Jesus, open my ears to truly hear my husband. Teach me to patiently pursue his heart by asking probing questions. Awaken my curiosity for all the unspoken treasures hidden in his heart and soul. Help me to honor what he shares with me and never use it as ammunition against him.

THE FRUIT OF ENCOURAGEMENT

"This challenge has been a blessing and opened both my eyes and my heart in areas of my marriage where there was huge room for improvement. It wasn't all smooth sailing and was very challenging on many days, as I'm just so bossy! There's a reason why I have two ears and only one mouth, so I'm waiting and listening before I speak and giving the Holy Spirit a chance to catch up with my runaway mouth."

REFLECT AND RESPOND

Ask your husband about something he is interested in and really listen to his answers.

Ask him about ways you could serve him better. (Don't try to apologize or justify yourself; just listen.)

Write down what he shared:

_____

_____

_____

_____

_____

_____

_____

GO DEEPER

Give your husband the gift of your attention and silence. Be careful not to bombard him with a lot of questions in order to make him speak. Instead, be diligent in expressing your interest and love. Let him respond first in social environments, and avoid contradicting him in public. Remember that your words don't prove your worth.

"
We need to express our
appreciation out loud.
Our husbands need to know
we value and love them.
"

Remember: You Chose Him

YOUR CHALLENGE:

- Don't say anything negative about your husband—to him or to anyone else about him.

- Tell your husband something you admire or appreciate about him—and say it to someone else about him!

VERSE

Behold, you are beautiful, my beloved, truly delightful.
—Song of Solomon 1:16

DEVOTIONAL

One of the things that first drew me to my husband was his sense of humor. I appreciated how he could laugh at himself and how we often found the same jokes funny. I also noticed early on his love and respect for his family and his desire to honor God with his words and actions.

These things are all still true of my husband. But twenty years into marriage, I don't voice my appreciation as much as I did in the early days. When was the last time I told him how much I appreciated his devotion to the Lord? Honestly, I don't remember.

Whether it's about the characteristics that first drew us to these men or things we've grown to appreciate over time, we need to express our appreciation out loud. Our husbands need to know we value and love them. They need to realize that we think they're special and want to pursue a deeper relationship with them.

Today, ask yourself, *What do I appreciate about my husband? How can I show him my admiration?* Then take the time to tell him!

—M.K.

PRAYER

Jesus, I confess that it's often easier to criticize than admire. Please remind me of the reasons why I chose my husband in the first place, and point out characteristics that I've been blind to. Help me speak words of admiration, and renew in me a deep, passionate love for my husband.

THE FRUIT OF ENCOURAGEMENT

"God used this challenge to transform my husband's and my relationship. Each day was extremely helpful. However, on Day 10 the Lord really spoke to me. As I did the 'Going Deeper' exercise, the Lord showed me that I was focusing so much on my husband's imperfections that I forgot what God originally intended him to be: a wonderful, generous gift. I had been taking this gift for granted and destroying our marriage in the process. Since then, I can't believe how much our marriage has turned around. Not only is my husband feeling more loved and appreciated, but deep in my heart I feel love and appreciation toward him, too."

What are some characteristics of your husband that drew you to him before you were married?

_____

_____

_____

_____

What are three things you appreciate about your husband right now?

_____

_____

_____

_____

What is one _practical_ way you can show your husband appreciation and admiration?

_____

_____

_____

_____

GO DEEPER

Think about the things that first drew you to your husband. Was it his sense of humor? His kind eyes? His love for the Lord? Then write him a love letter telling him all the things you appreciate and admire about him, and leave it on his pillow, on the breakfast table, or somewhere else he'll be sure to find it.

"A wife showcases the heart of Jesus—His love, sacrifice, and humility—when she willingly respects her husband."

Day 11

The Power of Respect

YOUR CHALLENGE:

- Don't say anything negative about your husband—to him or to anyone else about him.

- Tell your husband something you admire or appreciate about him—and say it to someone else about him!

VERSE

Wives, submit to your own husbands, as to the Lord.
—Ephesians 5:22

DEVOTIONAL

Some surprises are delightful; some just aren't.

Out of the blue, my predictable husband threw a monkey wrench into our plan for retirement. We'd recently downsized our home when he caught me off-guard by suggesting we move, yet again, to another town 100 miles away. Shocked and hurt, I refused to listen to his dream as the prospect of another move grew into a bone of contention in our marriage. After months of stubbornly resisting his leadership, the Lord reminded me of the truth of Ephesians 5:22: *Resistance to my husband is the same as resistance to Him.*

Part of showing respect to our husbands includes submitting to their authority: "For the husband is the head of the wife even as Christ is the head of the church, his body, and is himself its Savior" (Eph. 5:23).

To submit to your husband's leadership when you agree is a joyful task; when we prefer another way or believe a different way is wiser, it's tough. But look at it through the lens of the gospel. It's a glorious opportunity to reflect the way Jesus the Son submitted to God His Father. A wife showcases the heart of Jesus—His love, sacrifice, and humility—when she willingly respects her husband.

—L.B.

PRAYER

Father, forgive me for the times I subverted your pattern for marriage by disrespecting my husband. Lord, I need Your help to honor him as a way of honoring You. Give me the humility of Christ, who bowed His head to the Father. Transform our marriage into a vibrant picture of the gospel—Your relationship with Your Bride, the Church.

THE FRUIT OF ENCOURAGEMENT

"Praying for my husband has taken my marriage to another realm of contentment. We had been married for three years and were miserable. We were both Christians coming into our marriage, but we were both weak in having daily quiet times. I started to resent him because he was supposed to be the spiritual leader of our house. As I prayed over him and tried to encourage him more, he started to grow and get a desire to be in the Word. So much so, he had felt my prayers, and not knowing I was doing this challenge, he thanked me for praying for him. I honestly believe this saved our marriage."

REFLECT AND RESPOND

Make a list of characteristics you admire about your husband.

_____

_____

_____

_____

_____

_____

_____

_____

Find opportunities to verbally affirm these positive traits to him.

Ask God to reveal any areas that you're resisting your husband's leadership, then seek forgiveness—first from God, then from your husband.

GO DEEPER

Take time today to listen to your husband and affirm his leadership. Seek his input on decisions and challenges you're facing. Let him know you respect his opinions and welcome his wisdom, support, and love as your beloved partner. Take a bold step—the next time you're in public with your husband, find something to praise him for while people are listening.

" Don't give up, for 'at just
the right time we will reap a
harvest of blessing.'

"

Day 12

It's Time for a Heart Check!

YOUR CHALLENGE:

- Don't say anything negative about your husband—to him or to anyone else about him.

- Tell your husband something you admire or appreciate about him—and say it to someone else about him!

VERSE

Walk . . . with all humility and gentleness, with patience, bearing with one another in love. —Ephesians 4:1–2

DEVOTIONAL

Raise your hand if you've ever started a new exercise program and subconsciously expected to see results within just a few days. (Or maybe after a single workout.)

As I stretch my hand high into the sky, I realize it makes no sense. I know in my head that true change is going to take a while, and yet I somehow expect to see instant results.

Maybe you're in the same place today in this thirty-day challenge. Are you finding it difficult to encourage your husband? Has it been hard to check criticism and replace it with words of appreciation? Maybe you're thinking, *I've poured all this energy into my marriage, and things haven't changed a bit!*

Let's do a heart check! You may be doing everything exactly right, but the problem could lie within your own expectations. Just like

I secretly hope that the scale will plummet after I get done with my spinning class, you may be expecting too much too soon.

So, spend some time in prayer, asking God to show you if you have any unrealistic (or even unreasonable) expectations of your husband. And most importantly, don't give up, for "at just the right time we will reap a harvest of blessing" (Gal. 6:9 NLT).

—M.K.

PRAYER

Lord, search my heart for any ways I've been expecting too much from my husband. Help me come to You with my unmet needs, and teach me to trust You to work in my marriage—both in my husband and in my own heart. Help me to keep on doing good so that I will reap Your harvest of blessing.

THE FRUIT OF ENCOURAGEMENT

"This challenge was more wonderful and difficult than I could have believed. I thought I was an encouraging wife; I found out that I was not. It was actually humbling for me to continually encourage my husband for thirty days! God revealed in His great mercy my proud heart and the continual need for repentance. I plan on continuing this journey, doing it all over again until encouraging my husband becomes a habit. My husband's response to all the encouragement? All positive. He is more attentive and loving, plus he's been listening to me more."

REFLECT AND RESPOND

What unrealistic expectations have you been holding on to for your husband?

_____

_____

_____

_____

_____

_____

How can you let go of those expectations and look at your husband through eyes of grace?

_____

_____

_____

_____

_____

_____

GO DEEPER

Take some time to write down any changes you've seen so far during this challenge, even if they're miniscule. They could be in your husband or in you. Then verbally thank your husband for the things he is doing in your marriage, and release him from any overly demanding expectations the Lord has shown you.

"

God intended for marital
intimacy to be a vibrant and
regular expression of love.
Sex is God's idea, His good
gift for our marriage.

"

Day 13

Don't Settle for a Passionless Marriage

YOUR CHALLENGE:

- Don't say anything negative about your husband—to him or to anyone else about him.

- Tell your husband something you admire or appreciate about him—and say it to someone else about him!

VERSE

I am my beloved's, and his desire is for me. —Song of Solomon 7:10

DEVOTIONAL

A great sex life takes a lot of work; it doesn't happen naturally. So it's not surprising that many couples find tension and hurt in the bedroom rather than refreshment and joy. But God intended for marital intimacy to be a vibrant and regular expression of love. Sex is God's idea, His good gift for our marriage. So don't settle for a passionless marriage. Start praying that God would help you enjoy this gift and would show you what is standing in the way of enjoyment.

Negativity—toward our husbands or ourselves—kills intimacy. Start fighting for passion by showering your husband with encouragement. Communicate with words and actions that you enjoy being with him. Don't turn him away when he pursues you, but instead thank him for desiring you. Tell him what you appreciate about him as a lover. Be specific. Then fight for passion by casting aside your negative thoughts toward yourself—whether they are insecurities about your body, your personality, or anything else. Remember, most husbands genuinely long for intimacy with their wives. His desire is for you. So, be confident in his love.

For some, you may be more interested in sex than your husband. Don't be discouraged by this difficult situation! Know that God sees your situation and cares. Seek Him for wisdom and unity in this area, and look for other ways to have quality time and physical touch together. Be a good listener, and don't take anything too personally. Things likely won't change overnight, but keep showering your husband with encouragement and pray for him daily. There is always hope for those who trust in God.

—K.N.

PRAYER

Lord Jesus, no matter how I have struggled in the past, I don't want to settle for a passionless marriage. Free me from wrong thinking, and heal me from past sins and shame. Grow great desire in me for my husband and the confidence to pursue him and receive his pursuit of me. Give me wisdom to encourage my husband in this area—and please encourage my heart as well!

THE FRUIT OF ENCOURAGEMENT

"I started this challenge out of desperation, and now I can honestly say that my husband and I are experiencing real friendship, love, and respect for one another—even fun! And we have a significantly improved intimate life together, something I thought I was done with for the rest of my life. This challenge is just another example of how when I become willing, God changes my heart and my life."

REFLECT AND RESPOND

How can you affirm your husband as a lover today?

_____

_____

_____

_____

What thought patterns in this area of your life are not in line with the Truth?

_____

_____

_____

What's one way you can create some quality time with your husband today?

_____

_____

_____

_____

GO DEEPER

If you frequently shut down your husband's sexual advances, ask God to show you why you do this. Is it your work habits? Your parenting habits? An unwillingness to make time for date nights? You might consider apologizing to your husband for any discouragement your rejection may have caused. Find a way to demonstrate your desire for your husband today, maybe with a romantic note or a long kiss after he gets home. You are both bound to stumble as you take steps toward a passionate marriage, so be prepared to give grace for missteps and mistakes.

"
Consider all the ways a man
can show integrity, and praise
your husband for one of these
attributes he displays.
"

Day 14

A Man of Integrity

YOUR CHALLENGE:

- Don't say anything negative about your husband—to him or to anyone else about him.

- Tell your husband something you admire or appreciate about him—and say it to someone else about him!

VERSE

Whoever walks in integrity walks securely, but he who makes his ways crooked will be found out. —Proverbs 10:9

DEVOTIONAL

Living with integrity is challenging. Having right expectations about the world can prepare us to stand strong. Paul described what we can expect in 2 Timothy 3:2–5:

People will be lovers of self, lovers of money, proud, arrogant, abusive, disobedient to their parents, ungrateful, unholy, heartless, unappeasable, slanderous, without self-control, brutal, not loving good, treacherous, reckless, swollen with conceit, lovers of pleasure rather than lovers of God, having the appearance of godliness, but denying its power.

In a culture that is filled with all that sin, in what ways does your husband stand out?

Is he honest and fair with people? Does he show honor with his words and actions in your home, community, and church? How does he serve your family and others? Is he genuine in his faith? Consider all the ways a man can show integrity, and praise your husband for one of these attributes he displays.

As you continue in the 30-Day Husband Encouragement Challenge, look for ways that your husband stands against the culture with integrity.

—H.J.F

PRAYER

Heavenly Father, would You enable my husband to act justly, love mercy, and walk humbly with You? Let him be aware of weak spots around his mind and heart. Show him how to walk in integrity by fortifying his resolve through prayer, Your Word, and accountability. Protect him from evil. Show me how to praise and encourage him to stay strong in his actions.

THE FRUIT OF ENCOURAGEMENT

"My husband does not walk with the Lord, and we are going through an extremely difficult time. I was losing my joy in the marriage and my basic trust in his integrity. This challenge was a God-sent blessing. Daily I was encouraged, primarily by Scripture I knew but wasn't relying on. I had given the problems the power in my life. The challenge helped me put God back in control. I am much calmer, appreciating my husband more. He has responded to my re-found joy and encouragement."

REFLECT AND RESPOND

What is one way your husband's integrity has protected you or your marriage?

_____

_____

_____

_____

_____

_____

Do you see the impact of your husband's integrity on his friends or your children?

_____

_____

_____

_____

_____

_____

GO DEEPER

Pray regularly for your husband's sense of integrity, that he would be sensitive to the Spirit in all ways. As you have the opportunity—as it is appropriate—share examples of your husband's honesty and integrity with others. In particular, if you have children, point out his integrity to them. Your prayers and words will serve to strengthen him.

"If your husband isn't pursuing God or leading spiritually, turn to the Lord and trust Him to work in your husband's heart."

Day 15

His Pursuit of God

YOUR CHALLENGE:

- Don't say anything negative about your husband—to him or to anyone else about him.

- Tell your husband something you admire or appreciate about him—and say it to someone else about him!

VERSE

Grow in the grace and knowledge of our Lord and Savior Jesus Christ. —2 Peter 3:18

DEVOTIONAL

Encouraging your husband to pursue God is incredibly important. However, it takes discernment and humility to do this in a way that doesn't overstep your role as his wife. How can you encourage without leading?

One way is to ask how you can pray for him. Asking him to share specific requests shows that you care about what he cares about, and it can encourage him in his own prayers. If you have questions about Scripture, ask him for help instead of defaulting to a website or study guide. Show him that you value his thoughts in spiritual matters.

At times I have told my husband what I wished he would do to lead spiritually, which communicated that he wasn't measuring up in this area. I thought I was helping by giving suggestions. Instead, I was doing quite the opposite. If your husband isn't pursuing God or leading spiritually, turn to the Lord and trust Him to work in your husband's heart. It may be difficult to hold your tongue, but if you pray diligently, encourage him even in baby steps, and refrain from "helpful" suggestions, you will honor the Lord and avoid discouraging your husband.

—M.H.

PRAYER

Lord Jesus, more than anything else in my marriage, I want my husband to have a fruitful and growing relationship with You. Give him a desire for knowing and honoring You in every area of life. Forgive me for ways I have criticized his faith walk instead of encouraging him to pursue You. Thank You for loving him more than I do and wanting to be in relationship with him.

THE FRUIT OF ENCOURAGEMENT

"I've been a Christian for more than twenty years, but my husband doesn't share the same walk. Many times I've asked him to do Bible studies with me and he's always rejected the offers, so I know he doesn't really know Scripture to quote. This morning, I woke up and he just looked at me, stroked my face so gently, and started quoting Proverbs 31 over me—how precious I am to him, how I have always worked with him and loved him no matter what, how I've been good with finances, etc. My husband has never been that verbal with me before about his feelings. I believe this happened because I listened to your challenge and accepted it, and the Lord worked on me. He changed me and my attitude."

REFLECT AND RESPOND

Have you been encouraging your husband in his walk with God or trying to lead him spiritually by nagging?

_____

_____

_____

_____

_____

_____

Are you being faithful in pursuing God yourself?

_____

_____

_____

_____

_____

_____

GO DEEPER

Remember who your husband was when you first met? Has there been growth? If so, point that out to him. He may not realize how much God has done. If you honestly can't see any growth, keep praying and trusting and looking for ways to encourage his thoughts toward spiritual things in a way that isn't nagging or critical.

"

When you find it hard to
see your husband as a dear
companion, stop looking at
him and start looking at what
Christ has done for you.

Day 16

Your Life Companion

YOUR CHALLENGE:

- Don't say anything negative about your husband—to him or to anyone else about him.

- Tell your husband something you admire or appreciate about him—and say it to someone else about him!

VERSE

The LORD God said, "It is not good that the man should be alone; I will make him a helper fit for him." —Genesis 2:18

DEVOTIONAL

Loneliness is a problem, a big one. One study found that half of all Americans feel lonely. But God had a plan to combat loneliness from the beginning: each other. In marriage, that "each other" remedy is one man and one woman so intertwining their lives that they are one in God's eyes.

As sinners it's easy to focus on how our husbands fall short in being the companion we desire. When you find it hard to see your husband as a dear companion, stop looking at him and start looking at what Christ has done for you. Then take that mercy you've tasted and find some way to show your husband the friendship you desire.

My husband works on projects a lot. He would tell you he's a workaholic. And it can become easy for me to focus on the companionship we lack. But I've found with a steady diet of God's

Word, prayer, and remembrance of Christ's love for me, I can walk out to my husband in the midst of his projects, put my hand on his shoulder, playfully engage him with a little conversation and offer food or drink, and I am helped in remembering this man is just a man. Like me, he fails to be the ideal companion. But with mercy, we can walk through this hard life together.

—S.D.

PRAYER

Heavenly Father, forgive me for the tendency to focus on my husband's weaknesses rather than being the confidant and friend he can lean on for help and encouragement. Strengthen our unique connection as husband and wife, and help me discover ways to deepen our relationship.

THE FRUIT OF ENCOURAGEMENT

"This challenge has impacted my already 'good' marriage in a big way in just seven days. I've seen a huge leap in my husband's happiness in just seeing him smile and come home to a wife who shows her appreciation. I have always appreciated my husband but not in a way that was noticeable to everyone around. Through this challenge I've seen a turnaround in romance in my marriage and brought happiness to my very stressed husband. This was truly an answer to my prayers."

REFLECT AND RESPOND

During lonely times in your marriage, how can you find comfort in Christ?

_____

_____

_____

_____

_____

_____

In what ways could you meet your husband where he's at in order to deepen your connection?

_____

_____

_____

_____

_____

_____

GO DEEPER

Seek your husband as your life companion. Share little things and big news with him first. Make a point of planning time together, whether through an outing or time alone together at home, or join him in the activities he enjoys. Affirm the ways that he is your best friend and how you are happy God has given him to you as your life companion.

> We have hope—because
> God promises to give wisdom
> to the one who lacks it and
> asks for it with faith.

Day 17

The Home that Wisdom Builds

YOUR CHALLENGE:

- Don't say anything negative about your husband—to him or to anyone else about him.

- Tell your husband something you admire or appreciate about him—and say it to someone else about him!

VERSE

> *The fear of the LORD is the beginning of wisdom, and the knowledge of the Holy One is insight.* —Proverbs 9:10

DEVOTIONAL

As women, we are either building up or tearing down our home. The outcome is determined by whether we choose wisdom over foolishness (Prov. 14:1). In theory, no one wants to damage their family, but in real life it's so easy to conform our thoughts and desires to the world's foolishness.

True wisdom is only found in the Word of God, and it flows from fearing the Lord (Prov. 9:10). James 3:17 says that "[this type of] wisdom is first pure, then peaceable, gentle, open to reason, full of mercy and good fruits, impartial and sincere." Every time I read that passage I feel a strong conviction in my heart about my need to grow in godly wisdom. The good news is that we have hope—because God promises to give wisdom to the one who lacks it and asks for it with faith.

Without a doubt, your husband is one of the first people who will benefit from godly wisdom. He will be grateful if your way of living is pure, peaceable, gentle, open to reason, full of mercy and good fruits, impartial, and sincere. Don't you want to live that way? I know I do. So, let's run to the source of wisdom!

—B.G.

PRAYER

God, I run to You, confessing that I have been a fool in many ways. Give me a thirst for Your Word so I can discern the worldly patterns I have conformed to. Fill my heart with wonder and fear toward You, and help that filling to be evident in my relationship with my husband.

THE FRUIT OF ENCOURAGEMENT

"It's been amazing how the perfect occasion to take your suggestion to encourage my husband comes up each day. He has been on the defensive with me for the last several years, but today as we were working together and I asked him a question, he answered as though it was a simple question. It occurred to me that he was responding as though he was beginning to trust me again. You have given me the training and encouragement I need to be the kind of wife my husband needs."

REFLECT AND RESPOND

Is the way you interact with your husband more similar to James 3:14 or James 3:17?

_____

_____

Have you treated your husband in a foolish way?

_____

_____

_____

_____

_____

Would you dare to confess that treatment and ask for forgiveness?

_____

_____

_____

_____

GO DEEPER

Remember that a woman's godly wisdom is shown by her conduct and actions rather than just her speech. Be intentional in building up your husband with wise Christ-like service.

Do more than simply
partner with your husband
in the work assigned to you.
Enjoy him!

Day 18

Permission To Enjoy Each Other

YOUR CHALLENGE:

- Don't say anything negative about your husband—to him or to anyone else about him.

- Tell your husband something you admire or appreciate about him—and say it to someone else about him!

VERSE

A joyful heart is good medicine. —*Proverbs 17:22*

DEVOTIONAL

Age and responsibility tend to chip away at our playful sides. Who has time for fun when there is always so much to do?

And yet our relationships with our husbands have the potential to be pressure valves that release some of the built-up stress of daily life. Marriage can (and should!) be fun.

Consider:

- Are most conversations with your husband serious and task-centered?

- Do you thwart your husband's attempts at playfulness with rolled eyes or sharp words?

- For parents, do you encourage or discourage your husband's playful side with your children?

- What prevents you from simply *enjoying* your husband?

Listen to the invitation found in Scripture:

Enjoy life with the wife whom you love, all the days of your vain life that he has given you under the sun, because that is your portion in life and in your toil at which you toil under the sun. (Eccl. 9:9)

Do more than simply partner with your husband in the work assigned to you. *Enjoy him!* Watch for evidence of his playful side and play along. Look for opportunities to enjoy life together more often through games, hobbies, or experiences. What can you do today to initiate some fun?

—E.D.

PRAYER

Lord Jesus, so many times the pressure of life gets the better of me, and I take everything so seriously. Help me to rejoice in life, to be quick to laugh and find humor. Increase our joy, and make our marriage a place where we have fun and laugh together.

THE FRUIT OF ENCOURAGEMENT

"I took the 30-Day Husband Encouragement Challenge. It worked and is still working. It was an immediate turnaround for both of us. We are the best we have been in a long time. It's wonderful to enjoy my husband and laugh with him again. Even when we hit a couple of rough spots, we were able to turn them around quickly. I thank God for opening my ears up just at the moment you were speaking on the radio."

REFLECT AND RESPOND

Who tends to be more serious, you or your husband? Who tends to be more playful?

_____

_____

_____

_____

_____

_____

How can you grow in appreciation of your differences in temperament in this area?

_____

_____

_____

_____

_____

_____

GO DEEPER

Do something fun. Think of something lighthearted for you and your husband to do. Fly a kite, go for a bike ride, watch a funny movie, make silly faces—whatever you can think of to do to enjoy your husband today.

My beloved is radiant and
ruddy, distinguished among
ten thousand.

—Song of Solomon 5:10

Day 19

Fearfully and Wonderfully Made

YOUR CHALLENGE:

- Don't say anything negative about your husband—to him or to anyone else about him.

- Tell your husband something you admire or appreciate about him—and say it to someone else about him!

VERSE

My beloved is radiant and ruddy, distinguished among ten thousand.
—*Song of Solomon 5:10*

DEVOTIONAL

The first time I saw my husband, I thought, Wow, he's tall! At 6'5", he tends to stand out in most crowds. While I'm attracted to his long legs, I also love how his height makes me feel feminine and protected. And at my vertically-challenged 5'3", I'm happy to have someone help me reach the high cupboards!

Other physical features that I appreciate about my husband include his brilliant blue eyes, his wide and easy smile, his honest face, and his thick wavy hair. And when I make it a point to tell him the ways I find him physically attractive, I can see his eyes brighten, his smile grow bigger, and his stature increase to almost 6'6"!

When we share with our spouses the things we appreciate about them physically, it boosts their confidence and helps them feel closer to us. The opposite is true as well. Almost nothing is as devastating to a man as the belief that his wife doesn't find him attractive. If you ever criticize his body, those are words you can never take back.

So, take the time today to praise your husband's physical characteristics. Tell him you're glad God made his arms strong, his shoulders wide, his chest hairy, or whatever it is about him that you are attracted to. Let him know that you find him attractive and that you're glad he's your man.

—M.K.

PRAYER

Lord, thank You for how You made my husband. You're the One who knit him together and created him to be unique. Help me to appreciate the beauty of my husband's physical form in new ways. Forgive me for any times that I've been critical and for the ways I've aligned my expectations for physical appearance with our current cultural standards. Help me to be creative in letting my husband know that I'm attracted to him, and let that knowledge increase his confidence and strengthen our marriage.

THE FRUIT OF ENCOURAGEMENT

"I can't remember how I found this challenge, but I know it was out of desperation as I was becoming increasingly negative and could see how it was slowly eating at my marriage. It's only Day 13, but my heart is changing and I'm falling in love with my husband all over again. He doesn't know I'm doing this, but he is loving how I'm treating him and slowly but surely I am receiving the same in return. This challenge has helped me personally as well as in our marriage to reflect what God intended for us in the beginning."

REFLECT AND RESPOND

What physical characteristics do you admire in your husband? In what ways has God made him unique?

_____

_____

_____

_____

_____

_____

_____

What are some creative ways you could communicate to your husband that you find him physically attractive? If you're having a difficult time in this area, ask God to increase your attraction to your husband. Maybe it could start with appreciating his eyes, his smile, etc.

_____

_____

_____

_____

GO DEEPER

Read a wife's description of her beloved in Song of Solomon 5:10–16. Just as this woman did for her husband, take time to look over your husband's body, from the tip of his toes to his bald or bushy head, and thank God that he is "wonderfully made." Then send a flirtatious text message, leave him a love note, or tell him verbally how you find him attractive.

Forgive your husband because
God has forgiven *you*.

Day 20

Dig Out Bitter Roots

YOUR CHALLENGE:

- Don't say anything negative about your husband—to him or to anyone else about him.

- Tell your husband something you admire or appreciate about him—and say it to someone else about him!

VERSE

Be kind to one another, tenderhearted, forgiving one another, as God in Christ forgave you. —Ephesians 4:32

DEVOTIONAL

If you are unwilling to forgive your husband, you will find it difficult to encourage him. At this point in the thirty-day challenge, it's possible the Lord has exposed some areas of bitterness that are contaminating your relationship. Now is the time to deal with any unforgiving attitudes you've stored up. Forgive your husband, not because he hasn't hurt you or even because he's apologized or changed. Forgive your husband because God has forgiven *you*.

Hebrews 12:15 says, "See to it that no one fails to obtain the grace of God; that no 'root of bitterness' springs up and causes trouble, and by it many become defiled."

Bitterness within your marriage will produce a crop that will impact many: your husband, your children, your church, and your community. Invite God to tend to the soil of your heart in this area, expressing your desire to have all seeds of bitterness removed.

Is your husband a forgiving man? Does he keep short accounts of your problems? Express your thankfulness. Does your husband seem to harbor grudges against you? If so, do you need to ask forgiveness for an offense?

No matter how your husband handles his heart, you are called to freedom from bitter roots. Ask the Lord to remove all bitterness from your marriage so that you can walk in freedom in your relationship with Him and others.

—E.D.

PRAYER

Heavenly Father, I have sinned against You by judging and resenting my husband. Forgive me for being stingy with forgiveness when You have been so generous. Fill me with love and compassion for my husband.

THE FRUIT OF ENCOURAGEMENT

"About two months ago my husband and I began having problems communicating. This started a ball rolling in a direction we both did not want to go—anger, bitterness, resentment, discontentment, disconnect. I ran across this challenge months ago but never took the time to actually do it. I finally started it about fourteen days ago, and I cannot tell you the turnaround! We are communicating the problems we have with each other and actually have some kind of resolution in our conflicts."

REFLECT AND RESPOND

Can you think of times when your bitterness toward your husband impacted others outside your marriage?

_____

_____

_____

_____

_____

_____

In what ways is your bitterness hindering your freedom?

_____

_____

_____

_____

_____

GO DEEPER

Start digging. Ask the Lord to show you the roots of bitterness in your heart. Make a list of them, and ask God to forgive you for your resentment. Then choose to forgive your husband in response to God's extravagant forgiveness toward you.

"

Only two things will go
into eternity: the Word of
God and people. Be sure
you are focusing on the
right things—even in your
marriage relationship.

Day 21

Living for the Kingdom

YOUR CHALLENGE:

- Don't say anything negative about your husband—to him or to anyone else about him.

- Tell your husband something you admire or appreciate about him—and say it to someone else about him!

VERSE

"But seek first the kingdom of God and his righteousness, and all these things will be added to you." —Matthew 6:33

DEVOTIONAL

If we are living in light of eternity, everything we think, do, or say is seen from an eternal perspective. Only two things will go into eternity: the Word of God and people. Be sure you are focusing on the right things—even in your marriage relationship.

Does your husband have an eternal perspective that allows him to reject momentary pleasures, materialism, and temporal values? Does he seek God's glory instead of his own? Express your gratitude for your husband's value system, and praise him for putting God's kingdom and eternal things before the things of this world.

If this is a problem area for him, consider how you might alter your own value system and live for eternity in front of him, encouraging him to do the same. Determine today that your words will build your husband up, encouraging him to live for God's kingdom.

—H.J.F.

PRAYER

Jesus, I want to be a wise steward by investing in eternal things. Help my husband and me to see where we need to adjust our thinking and priorities. Then enable us to actively pursue the work and relationships You have for us, so that our lives are centered on Your kingdom values.

THE FRUIT OF ENCOURAGEMENT

"My husband and I have been married thirty-one years, and I thought I was a very encouraging wife. Then I completed this challenge. The changes in my husband and me were remarkable. After only five or six encouraging statements to my husband on different days, he was just beaming! His whole demeanor changed. I was so convicted for how I have taken my husband for granted and only let my mind dwell on how he could improve and what he could do better. I'm doing this challenge again so it becomes a habit!"

REFLECT AND RESPOND

What strengths does your husband have that might be used to grow
God's kingdom? How can you encourage him in those strengths?

_____

_____

_____

_____

_____

_____

What issues or groups of people is your husband particularly drawn to
and compassionate toward?

_____

_____

_____

_____

_____

GO DEEPER

Assess any habits or patterns in your life that aren't prioritizing God's
Word and people. Make adjustments to honor God and focus your home
more on the kingdom.

"Men and women are very
different, and God made it
that way. We're meant to
complement each other,
not be identical."

Day 22

Season Your Speech with Grace

YOUR CHALLENGE:

- Don't say anything negative about your husband—to him or to anyone else about him.

- Tell your husband something you admire or appreciate about him—and say it to someone else about him!

VERSE

Let your speech always be gracious. —*Colossians 4:6*

DEVOTIONAL

My husband is not (yet) a believer in Christ, and so the words of Colossians 4:6 feel very applicable. The context for this verse is the one right before it: "Walk in wisdom toward outsiders, making the best use of the time" (v. 5). Paul wants Christians to live and speak with grace toward those who have not put their hope in Christ.

Maybe that's your husband, but even if it's not, our husbands can at times feel like "outsiders." Men and women are very different, and God made it that way. We're meant to complement each other, not be identical. But the differences in the way we see the issues of life, even if we both trust in Christ, can make efforts at walking in unity seem overwhelming.

One way we can address these differences is by seasoning them with grace. The rest of Colossians 4:6 compares gracious speech to food seasoned with salt. Sometimes trying to come alongside our husbands amidst our differences can feel like trying to eat bland, unseasoned food. But gracious words such as, "I love it when you _____," or "I notice how hard you work and I appreciate you," or even "I'm so glad you're _____; you help me to see life from a different point of view," can make all the difference. When you fill in the blanks with gracious words, it will compliment the good "flavor" of your husband.

—S.D.

PRAYER

Father, forgive me for being so quick to point out my husband's differences as though they were wrong or bad. Help me love the different flavors of personality my husband brings to our marriage. Help me find ways to speak graciously to him so he will see Christ more clearly even through me.

THE FRUIT OF ENCOURAGEMENT

"I am on Day 14 of the challenge. On Day 3, my husband said, 'Thank you for staying off my back the past few days.' On Day 10, he brought me a dozen roses. When I asked why, he replied, 'Because you have been so cooperative and not pushed. You are so understanding.' He is not a believer, but this is truly making an impact on him."

REFLECT AND RESPOND

How does it encourage you to see the differences between you and your husband as complementary rather than as competing with each other?

_____

_____

_____

_____

_____

_____

What words could you fill in the blanks above with to encourage your husband this week?

_____

_____

_____

_____

_____

GO DEEPER

Use the fill-in-the-blank statements above to communicate a gracious message to your husband and find ways to show unmerited favor and kindness to him with your words. Remember the kindness and grace of God extended toward you even while you were still His enemy who disregarded His Son. Let the grace He gave to you be on your lips when you speak to your husband.

Each has his own gift

from God, one of one kind

and one of another.

—1 Corinthians 7:7

Day 23

Appreciating His Strengths

YOUR CHALLENGE:

- Don't say anything negative about your husband—to him or to anyone else about him.

- Tell your husband something you admire or appreciate about him—and say it to someone else about him!

VERSE

Each has his own gift from God, one of one kind and one of another.
—*1 Corinthians 7:7*

DEVOTIONAL

Whether our husbands share our faith in Christ or not, we should be able to recognize the gifts and talents God has given them. And most likely, the gifts He gave them are different than the ones He gave us. Often He will draw together two people with opposite strengths and weaknesses on purpose to refine and help us. Rather than focusing on our husbands' weaknesses, we should affirm their strengths.

Is your husband organized? Is he diligent? Is he persistent? These are all related to a pattern of personal discipline that are worthy of your praise—even when his bent for order and discipline comes against your bent for whimsy. Affirm him for these traits and how this helps your marriage function.

It can be easy to think we know our husbands pretty well—and we probably do know them better than most. But that shouldn't keep us from always learning about and being students of their hearts and personalities. Instead of approaching our husbands with the assumption we have them figured out, let's study them, recognize the things they're good at, and look for ways we can build them up.

—S.D.

PRAYER

Father, when I see the differences between my husband and me, sometimes I am grateful, but sometimes it's difficult. Let me serve my husband in love, with the gifts You've given me. Help me learn from my husband and lean on his strengths. Fill me today with an appreciation for how You've wired him, and help me to be a student of his heart so that I can praise him and build him up.

THE FRUIT OF ENCOURAGEMENT

"I figured I would give this challenge a try when a friend posted it on Facebook because what did I have to lose? It proved to be better than any marriage conference or advice I have ever received. You see, I have a great man, but I didn't know it. This challenge brought out new strengths in my husband every single day. I feel so bad that I never appreciated him before. He was right there beside me, but I didn't see. God is good and faithful to open my eyes. Today is Day 30, and tomorrow I am going to start over and do it all again. My marriage of eighteen years was hanging on; now it is awesome."

REFLECT AND RESPOND

What are your husband's strengths? How do they complement your weaknesses?

_____

_____

_____

_____

_____

How can you be a student of your husband today so that you're able to encourage him?

_____

_____

_____

_____

_____

GO DEEPER

You're over seventy-five percent of the way done with this challenge! Hopefully, it's getting easier to find ways to encourage your husband each day. But if not, ask God to give you fresh inspiration each day.

Today, think about the strengths God has given your husband, as well as those He's gifted to you. Find ways to use the abilities God has given you to serve your husband in love. Often we think of the good of missionary work or caring for the homeless or orphans—all good works God may have us do, but it is just as much a good work to love your husband right where you are and serve him so that he will be drawn to Christ.

Dear God, You are our
good Father. Thank You for
my husband and the ways he
reflects Your love.

Day 24

A Father at Heart

YOUR CHALLENGE:

- Don't say anything negative about your husband—to him or to anyone else about him.

- Tell your husband something you admire or appreciate about him—and say it to someone else about him!

VERSE

Fathers, do not provoke your children to anger, but bring them up in the discipline and instruction of the Lord. —Ephesians 6:4

DEVOTIONAL

I didn't grow up with my father, so my first interaction with an actual father at home was with my husband. When we were newlyweds, I was intrigued about the type of father he would become, and nowadays it amazes me to see him being a godly father instructing our children in the Lord.

What's sad, however, is that even though I highly respect him as a father, it's easy for me to spot his weaknesses and point them out without grace. I need to be very careful! My heart is deceitful and is always trying to convince me that I have a better explanation for the kids than he does, or that because I spend more time with them, I know what's best. Bottom line, I think I can do it better. This is the sinful seed of pride bearing fruit.

Sisters, we need grace to encourage our husbands in their role as fathers. We need to cultivate humility in order to allow our spouses' leadership to flourish in our homes. If you have children, let your husband take the lead and celebrate him for doing it. If you don't, then thank him for the ways he reflects God's character to the children around you.

—B.G.

PRAYER

Dear God, You are our good Father. Thank You for adopting us into Your family, sustaining us with Your grace, and providing faithfully. Thank You for my husband and the ways he reflects Your love as a father. Help him cling to You, and help me support him and submit to his leadership.

THE FRUIT OF ENCOURAGEMENT

"I want to thank you for the 30-day challenge to be an encourager to my husband. In our twenty-five years of marriage, I have found myself sometimes losing awareness of what a kind, loving husband and father he is, focusing instead on shortcomings or areas I was irritated about. This challenge has helped me to again see how blessed I am to have him as my husband."

Are you supporting your husband's leadership with your children or competing with it?

_____

_____

_____

_____

What, if any, attitudes do you need to change in order to foster a more supportive environment for him to grow as a father?

_____

_____

_____

_____

_____

_____

Are you willing to surrender those things to the Lord and ask for forgiveness?

GO DEEPER

Our children are witnesses of whether we support our husbands in their role as fathers or not. Sometimes an example is worth more than words. If the Lord convicts you of any sin in this matter, are you willing to ask for forgiveness to your husband in front of your kids? This could be a perfect opportunity for you to affirm him as a father.

"

Help both my husband and
me pursue peace so You are
magnified in our marriage.

"

Day 25

Making Peace a Priority

YOUR CHALLENGE:

- Don't say anything negative about your husband—to him or to anyone else about him.

- Tell your husband something you admire or appreciate about him—and say it to someone else about him!

VERSE

Seek peace and pursue it. —Psalm 34:14

DEVOTIONAL

Peace is something we may take for granted when it's present, but we sorely miss when it's lacking. Romans 12:18 says, "If possible, so far as it depends on you, live peaceably with all." That middle clause is an acknowledgment that sometimes peace is lacking despite our best efforts, but it also challenges us to do everything possible to achieve peace.

Your marriage may be characterized by peace, or arguments may be prominent. Either way, it's crucial to examine yourself to see if you are making peace a priority. Once you've determined that your heart genuinely seeks peace, you can begin to encourage your husband.

Maybe he is already a great peacemaker. Thank him for this and tell him how valuable his heart for peace is in your marriage. Does he handle conflict in other relationships with grace and humility? Encourage him in that, mentioning specific instances when he pursued peace. If, instead, he is more prone to angry confrontation, ask the Lord for wisdom in how to encourage him to prioritize peace more. Your example of seeking peace and refusing to fight will be its own encouragement, without you having to say a word.

—*M.H.*

PRAYER

Jesus, You are the Prince of Peace, and I long for peace to flourish in my heart, marriage, and home. Guard my tongue and my mind from divisive or angry words and attitudes. Help both my husband and me pursue peace so You are magnified in our marriage.

THE FRUIT OF ENCOURAGEMENT

"I can't explain how this happened, but I made a commitment to speaking good words to my husband for thirty days, and I experienced a big change on the first week—from him telling me how beautiful I look to bringing flowers after his day of work. It is like when we were dating eight years ago."

REFLECT AND RESPOND

Think about your words, tones, and attitudes. Are you creating an environment of peace in your home?

_____

_____

_____

_____

_____

_____

_____

"A soft answer turns away wrath, but a harsh word stirs up anger" (Prov. 15:1). Consider memorizing this verse and asking the Lord to soften your tongue in the midst of conflict.

GO DEEPER

I heard of a couple who each listed ten irritating things their spouse was likely to do, like leaving clothes on the floor or being late. They then promised to never argue or complain about anything on those lists. Imagine how this exercise might affect your marriage. Consider making such a list and committing to prioritize peace in each situation.

We shouldn't focus only on
our marriages but on pleasing
the Lord in all we do.

Day 26

Strike a Balance

YOUR CHALLENGE:

- Don't say anything negative about your husband—to him or to anyone else about him.

- Tell your husband something you admire or appreciate about him—and say it to someone else about him!

VERSE

Jesus increased in wisdom and in stature and in favor with God and man. —Luke 2:52

DEVOTIONAL

In a recent meeting with our church staff, my pastor talked about the myth of balance. To illustrate his point, he used guitar strings as a visual of this reality of life: tension. Life isn't so much about striking a balance; instead, it's striking a chord with constantly adjusted tensions. When we try to balance our life, we inevitably find that it's like trying to balance a teeter-totter by running from one side to the other. In Luke 2:52, we see Jesus striking a healthy tension between favor with God and favor with man. The same tension must be sought after in our relationships with our husbands.

As followers of Christ who are also married, we'll experience a tension between our desires to serve God and our desires to have great relationships with our husbands. Marriage is a gift from God, and we should honor it, stay faithful to our vows, and seek to glorify God in how we love our husbands. But while we tune the strings of our lives to bring a beautiful sound to God's ears, our marriages shouldn't compete with tuning the strings of growing in faith in and love toward God.

As Paul says in 1 Corinthians 7, we shouldn't focus only on our marriages but on pleasing the Lord in all we do. When we tune our lives with a healthy tension like Jesus, we grow in favor with God and man and strike a sort of balance that otherwise could never be achieved.

—S.D.

PRAYER

Father, help me to follow Jesus' lead in loving my husband and in growing in my love for You. Help me to seek first Your kingdom and Your righteousness, and by doing so, may I love my husband even more. Give me wisdom as I live out the tensions of life so that You would be glorified in my life and in my marriage.

THE FRUIT OF ENCOURAGEMENT

"While my marriage is good, I was stuck in a comfort zone. This challenge was just what I needed to appreciate my husband all over again! He works hard for myself and our daughters, keeps the yard well maintained, and is happily active in our lives, just to name a few. Your challenge has opened my eyes to stop taking all of that (and more) for granted! And if I can continue to thank him, especially in front of our girls, what a great witness that will be for them in their marriages one day."

REFLECT AND RESPOND

What tensions do you feel between serving God and growing your relationship with your husband? Are there areas where you need to make adjustments?

_____

_____

_____

_____

_____

_____

How can seeking God first help with achieving balance in your marriage and other areas of life?

_____

_____

_____

_____

_____

_____

GO DEEPER

Take time to consider how you handle the tension between your service to the Lord and your relationship with your husband. Are there times when you put your husband before your time with the Lord? Are there ways you might be serving at church that are causing you to neglect your marriage? Ask God to give you wisdom so that you are "tuning" your life and marriage to the melody He desires for you.

"
Keep your eyes on God, and
wait on Him to bring about
the changes you hope to see
in your marriage. He will not
disappoint you.

"

Day 27

Acknowledge His Courage

YOUR CHALLENGE:

Don't say anything negative about your husband—to him or to anyone else about him.

Tell your husband something you admire or appreciate about him—and say it to someone else about him!

VERSE

Be strong, and let your heart take courage, all you who wait for the Lord! —Psalm 31:24

DEVOTIONAL

You have almost completed the 30-Day Husband Encouragement Challenge! Perhaps it has taken a tremendous amount of courage to refrain from criticism and consistently speak words of encouragement to your husband. This kind of courage is only possible when we trust God and wait on Him. And it's this kind of courage we want to look for and celebrate in our husbands.

Courage isn't being a "tough guy," and it isn't the absence of fear and anxiety. Courage is at work when someone does the right thing despite the presence of fear, anxiety, and negative consequences. Where do you see your husband doing the right thing even though it hurts? Does he stand up for the rights of others, even when it's unpopular? Does he work hard to change injustice? Is he a stickler for the truth? Does he experience losses to protect you or your family? Point out the ways he is courageous and has been in the past, and thank him for setting an example for you.

And ask God for the courage you need today. Keep your eyes on God, and wait on Him to bring about the changes you hope to see in your marriage. Like the holy women who didn't "fear anything that was frightening," keep hoping in God (1 Peter 3:1–6). He will not disappoint you.

—K.N.

PRAYER

Father, thank You for the way my husband cares for our family and others. I am grateful for every expression of courage in him, whether big or small. Help me see new ways to strengthen him with my words and build him up. Whenever he is afraid or anxious, help him trust You and lean on Your strength.

THE FRUIT OF ENCOURAGEMENT

"I've been praying the prayers now for twenty-nine days, and I can tell you, restoration has begun. My husband and I have been separated for a total of eighteen years. Our children are grown now. But we serve an awesome God. My husband is on his way home!"

REFLECT AND RESPOND

What displays of courage might you be overlooking in your husband?

_____

_____

_____

_____

_____

_____

What causes your husband the most anxiety and fear?

_____

_____

_____

_____

_____

_____

Spend time today praying specifically for God to supply courage to him in that area.

GO DEEPER

Does your husband have a favorite wartime movie? One that celebrates the sacrificial courage of men? Why not suggest watching it together and then take some time after the movie to affirm the courage you see in your husband. If your husband is facing a particularly fearful season, write him a letter telling him how you are praying for him and that you are behind him 100 percent, cheering him on. Openly praise any evidence of your husband's courage in protecting you, your marriage, your family, or your home.

" A humble man is a
trustworthy and safe man,
but not often the type of man
our culture celebrates. "

Day 28

The Beauty of Humility

YOUR CHALLENGE:

- Don't say anything negative about your husband—to him or to anyone else about him.

- Tell your husband something you admire or appreciate about him—and say it to someone else about him!

VERSE

The fear of the LORD is instruction in wisdom, and humility comes before honor. —Proverbs 15:33

DEVOTIONAL

Humility is a difficult quality to walk out because it requires relinquishing our rights. Humility enables us to honor our husbands when we know they are wrong. Humility empowers us to refuse to retaliate when we feel hurt by our husbands. Humility fits our mouths with words of affirmation when we're tempted to criticize. Finish this month strong by asking for an extra dose of humility today. Remember, God gives grace to the humble (1 Peter 5:5).

Now, ask the Lord to help you see the humility in your husband. Does he willingly celebrate the victories of others without boasting about his own? Is he able to learn from others at work or church or elsewhere? Does he submit to the Word of God with joy? Does he set aside his preferences for the sake of others? Is he open about his failures and his need for God's grace? Today, point out and celebrate any expression of humility you've seen in your husband, no matter how small.

A humble man is a trustworthy and safe man, but not often the type of man our culture celebrates. So, let your husband know how meaningful his expressions of humility are to you and what a privilege it is to be married to a man who values this Christ-like characteristic. Thank him for setting an example for you to follow.

—K.N.

PRAYER

Father, give me strength to humble myself today. Show me areas of hidden pride, and give me grace to confess my pride to my husband and seek his forgiveness. Give me eyes that search for expressions of humility in my husband today rather than failures or shortcomings. Help me lay aside my rights as You did, Lord Jesus, and serve my husband with joy today.

THE FRUIT OF ENCOURAGEMENT

"Originally, I'd planned to tell my husband about this challenge at its end, but as it draws to a close I'm not sure that I will. I think I'll just keep telling him what I told him on Day 3. He asked, 'Why are you being so sweet and nice to me these past couple of days?' And I answered, 'Oh, the Lord's just working on my heart concerning you and our marriage, and I'm striving by His grace to not take either for granted ever again.'"

REFLECT AND RESPOND

What rights are you clinging to in your marriage?

_____

_____

_____

_____

_____

What past hurts or failures are you holding onto?

_____

_____

_____

_____

_____

Spend a moment releasing these to God, and read Philippians 2:5–8 while praying for God to give you the humble attitude of Christ.

GO DEEPER

Don't wait for a momentous display of humility to praise it in your husband. Look for the smallest, seed-like form of it, and praise it in him. Search the Bible for verses on humility, and write them in a card for your husband, sharing with him how grateful you are for his humility in specific ways.

> Through the enabling power
> of the Holy Spirit, you'll be
> able to walk in a manner
> worthy of our calling.

Day 29

Standing for Righteousness

YOUR CHALLENGE:

- Don't say anything negative about your husband—to him or to anyone else about him.

- Tell your husband something you admire or appreciate about him—and say it to someone else about him!

VERSE

Whoever pursues righteousness and kindness will find life, righteousness, and honor. —Proverbs 21:21

DEVOTIONAL

As you near the end of this challenge, take time to think about your husband's responses to the wickedness of culture, media, and the world. Does your husband recognize and turn away from evil? In what ways is he pursuing righteousness—living according to the standards of God in his covenantal relationships with Him and with you?

Understanding that sin is first and foremost against God should prompt us to walk in righteousness instead, like Joseph in the Old Testament, who fled from the wicked advances of Potiphar's wife (Gen. 39:9). Seek to know more of God's character and His ways with your husband. From a short discussion about your pastor's message in the car on the way home from church to reading through a book of the Bible together, there are many ways you can help each other better understand

God's righteousness. Then, through the enabling power of the Holy Spirit, you'll be able to walk in a manner worthy of our calling (Eph. 4:1).

—H.J.F

PRAYER

Heavenly Father, strengthen my husband's resolve to stand strong against the world, the flesh, and the devil. Protect him from evil, and remind him of his need for Your help to flee it and walk in righteousness. Keep him hungry for You so that nothing else satisfies. Help me to praise his choices that honor You.

THE FRUIT OF ENCOURAGEMENT

"This challenge helped to restore a balance in my relationship with my husband that was on the verge of falling. It brought new meaning and better perspectives into our relationship that we thought were lost. It helped me get through tough and painful times, and I thank God for every day He listened to my prayers. Day 30 was bittersweet—I was glad to have made it that far and thankful to be in a relationship with my husband but sad that I had reached the end."

REFLECT AND RESPOND

Can you remember a specific time when your husband promoted righteousness in your home?

_____

_____

_____

_____

_____

_____

Do you see righteousness in the lives of those around you?

_____

_____

_____

_____

Talk about those positive examples with your husband to encourage both of your hearts.

GO DEEPER

Praise your husband when he recognizes and turns his back on wickedness. If you can think of a situation where your husband stood for righteousness, remind him of that today—and express your gratitude. And pray that he would have the courage to stand for righteousness and that his example would leave a lasting impact in your family.

God is the One who first
brought you together, and He
can deepen and breathe new
life in your relationship
with your spouse.

Day 30

Cultivating Your Friendship

YOUR CHALLENGE:

- Don't say anything negative about your husband—to him or to anyone else about him.

- Tell your husband something you admire or appreciate about him—and say it to someone else about him!

VERSE

This is my beloved and this is my friend. —Song of Solomon 5:16

DEVOTIONAL

One of the best pieces of advice my mother ever gave me was that I should not only love the man I married, but I should also consider him to be my friend. I took this advice to heart. My husband and I were friends for a year before we ever dated, and we've continued to cultivate this friendship. Over the years, that has meant participating in activities we both enjoy, laughing over funny YouTube videos, praying together, and setting aside time to share about our days—the highs, the lows, and the mundane.

This friendship doesn't always come easy. When we've been apart for extended periods of time, are in a rough season, or feel the strain of living in a sinful world, it can be easy to drift apart. So, we have to be intentional about making any needed course corrections to get our relationship—and our friendship—back on track.

As you end this 30-Day Husband Encouragement Challenge, think about ways you can cultivate your friendship with your husband. Don't assume he knows that you value this aspect of your relationship; let him know he is both your sweetheart and your best friend.

If you're feeling distant from your husband, pray that God would help you connect in new ways. God is the One who first brought you together, and He can deepen and breathe new life in your relationship with your spouse.

—M.K.

PRAYER

Jesus, thank You for the friendship You've given me with my husband—for taking our two separate lives, making us "one flesh," and enabling us to understand each other in ways that no one else can. Thank You for how You've used these last thirty days in our marriage. May the blessings we've experienced as a result of this challenge grow. Continue to deepen my love for my husband, that he may know he is my beloved and my friend.

THE FRUIT OF ENCOURAGEMENT

"I have been touched and truly blessed by the 30-Day Husband Challenge. I realize how precious and integral my communication style is to our marriage. I recognize that our marriage is only as sweet as I am to him. As I continue this journey through God's Word, I want to be a wife after God's own heart. Thanks for helping me realize how vital my words are to my husband's well-being."

REFLECT AND RESPOND

How would you rate the closeness of your friendship with your husband?

_____

_____

_____

What are ways you could intentionally develop this aspect of your relationship?

_____

_____

_____

What are the benefits of having your husband be your best friend?

_____

_____

_____

_____

_____

GO DEEPER

Talk with your husband and together think of ways to deepen your friendship. It could include doing something fun together away from your normal responsibilities, reading a book and having a spirited discussion over the content, or praying together every night before you go to bed. Since every couple is unique, this process will look different for every marriage. Intentionally set aside time to make it happen.

The Challenge Continues

Dear Friends,

It's been a joy to be a part of your life each day to consider Truth together. This challenge may be over, but the adventure of growing in Truth isn't.

Revive Our Hearts has a simple mission—calling women to freedom, fullness, and fruitfulness in Christ. Everything we do, including this challenge, flows from a desire to see you thrive in your walk with Christ.

As we think of you, the words Christ prayed in the Garden of Gethsemane come to mind: "Sanctify them in the truth; your word is truth" (John 17:17).

God's Word changes us. So, let's continue to turn to God's Word together in the days ahead.

ReviveOurHearts.com is loaded with resources to help you do just that. Including . . .

Practical, biblical posts on our blogs:

- Find truth for every season of life at TrueWoman.com.

- Read posts by leaders for leaders on the Leader Connection blog.

- Learn how to help young women identify lies and replace them with God's Truth at LiesYoungWomenBelieve.com.

Meaningful Bible studies like:

- *Abigail: Living with the Difficult People in Your Life*

- *Elizabeth: Dealing with Disappointment*

- *Esther: Trusting God's Plan*

- *A Place of Quiet Rest: Finding Intimacy with God Through a Daily Devotional Life*

- *Seeking Him: Experiencing the Joy of Personal Revival*

We also have daily audio content created to help you thrive in Christ. Find out more at ReviveOurHearts.com. Our hope is for you to really know Him and to trust Him enough to obey, love, and enjoy Him. Let's keep turning toward Him together.

Blessings,

The *Revive Our Hearts* Team

Meet The Writers

Leslie Bennett

Leslie lives in the Lowcountry of South Carolina, where she never gets tired of watching spectacular sunsets, walking beside live oaks draped in Spanish moss, and drinking sweet tea on her front porch swing (with lemon, of course!). After thirty-six years of marriage, Leslie swears there's still something new to learn about your husband!

Erin Davis

Erin lives on a sheep farm in the Midwest. She likes growing green beans, playing dominoes with her family, and hanging out with her church small group. She married her husband, Jason, barefoot on the beach nearly twenty years ago. Since then, she's learned that marriage isn't about her and that love thrives in the soil of sacrifice.

Sheila Dougal

Sheila lives in Phoenix but is originally from a small town in Oregon. She likes crafting soap, reading a good biography, writing poetry, journaling, and taking long walks on cool days. For over twenty-five years, God has worked in her marriage to demonstrate His faithfulness and to let her taste the joy that comes from following Christ and humbling yourself to love another for His glory.

Heidi Jo Fulk

Heidi has lived in Michigan most of her twenty years of marriage. She and her husband have discovered various ways to connect through the years, through the stages of dating, being newly married, and parenting young and older children. They are committed to connecting together to strengthen their family and put Christ on display.

Betsy Gómez

Betsy lives in the Dallas area with her husband, Moisés, and their three children. She is a fan of good conversations around food and loves opening her home to foster community. She and her husband enjoy family movie nights and going on roadtrips. For fourteen years, they've seen the power of the gospel at work in their marriage and the beauty of trusting God no matter what.

Monica Hall

Monica makes her home in a rural community in the Bible Belt. She spends her days homeschooling and chauffeuring her kiddos, scouting out potential road trips, and looking for her next author to binge-read. Lately, God's been showing her more clearly the importance of finding practical, creative ways to help her husband, including anything from researching eschatology with him to walking his puppy every morning.

Mindy Kroesche

Mindy lives in a small city in the Midwest with her husband and two kids, but she's a country girl at heart. She likes relaxing at the lake with her family, curling up with a cozy mystery, and finding out what coffee shops serve the best raspberry mochas. Married to her best friend for twenty years, God daily shows her the importance of not taking her husband for granted and of being his biggest cheerleader.

Kelly Needham

Kelly Needham lives in the Dallas area with her husband and three kids. On her day off, you can find her working on a jigsaw puzzle, reading a novel, or chatting with a good friend. After twelve years of marriage, she still needs the reminder to hold back words of criticism and correction and instead speak words of encouragement and gratitude.

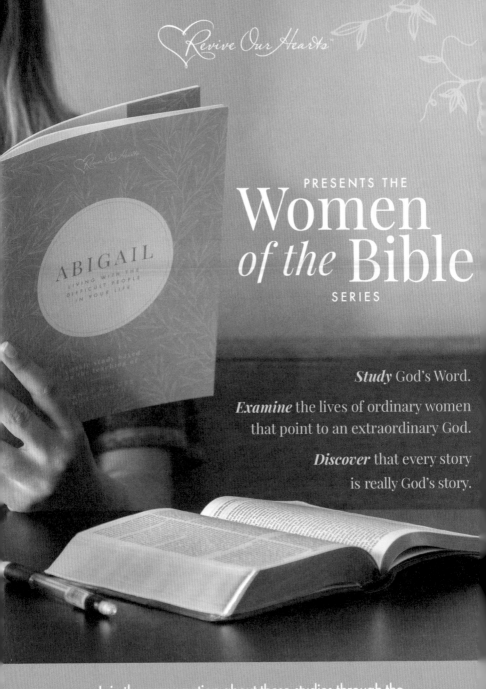

Revive Our Hearts™

PRESENTS THE

Women
of the Bible

SERIES

ABIGAIL
LIVING WITH THE
DIFFICULT PEOPLE
IN YOUR LIFE

Study God's Word.

Examine the lives of ordinary women
that point to an extraordinary God.

Discover that every story
is really God's story.

Join the conversation about these studies through the
Women of the Bible podcast. Listen in as women open God's
Word and walk through each study together.

REVIVEOURHEARTS.COM/WOMENOFTHEBIBLE

MORE FROM

Revive Our Hearts™

RADIO   •   EVENTS   •   BLOGS

LEADERS

REVIVE OUR **HEARTS** . COM